My Life

and

Times

My Life

and

Times

Douglas Smith

authorHOUSE®

AuthorHouse™ UK Ltd.
1663 Liberty Drive
Bloomington, IN 47403 USA
www.authorhouse.co.uk
Phone: 0800.197.4150

Published by AuthorHouse   12/16/2013

ISBN: 978-1-4918-8853-7 (sc)
ISBN: 978-1-4918-8852-0 (hc)
ISBN: 978-1-4918-8854-4 (e)

Contents

To Rosalind:

Without whose tuition and advice
this would not have been possible.

"And this our life exempt from public haunt
Finds tongues in trees, books in the running brooks,
Sermons in stones and good in everything.
I would not change it".

(As You Like It. Act 2, Scene 1)

55 High Street, Princes End, Tipton, Staffordshire, Sunday afternoon, February 3rd, 1924, 4 p.m. (just in time for tea), a weakly little boy came bawling into the world.

My sister Margery Gwendoline then 4 years old, on being asked to come and look at her new little brother said that she did not want a brother. (Sibling rivalry established at one hour old!).

Having been born into the combined families Smith and Douglass, and the Smith head male line apparently always being called Alfred, it was inevitable that my name would be Alfred Douglas Smith.

Our Grandparents were Alfred and Elizabeth Smith, (Granny Smith nee Jennings), and Abraham (Abram) John and Louisa Douglass, (Granny Douglass nee Loach).

Douglas Smith

The Smiths lived at Bank Street, Bradley, near Bilston, Staffs. and had seven surviving children, namely James, Alfred, George, Lizzie, Elsie, Alice and Evelyn.

The Douglasses had lived in Moat Road in another part of Tipton, but by the time I arrived we were living with them at No. 55. This was on the main road from Dudley to Wednesbury and had a tram service running for several years until just before the Second World War. As an aside, my Granny Douglass was in a crash on one of the trams and lost the sight of one eye thereby. No compensation in those days of course.

Two years later, after suffering Whooping Cough, when they despaired of my surviving ("You could see his little bones sticking out") my other sister Ruby Lilian came on the scene. We had a happy (mostly) childhood and apart from Measles when Dr. Murdoch gave us some lovely medicine that must have been something like Raspberry juice (and I remember Jaffa oranges and Arrowroot biscuits), it seems in retrospect that the sun was always shining.

Smith Family Portrait

I am told that in a tantrum because I wanted to ride in Marge's doll's pram, I threw out her doll, breaking it. I don't remember the occasion and I can only offer belated apologies!

Granny and Grandad Douglass also had quite a few children, several of whom died in childhood,—those surviving to adults were Harry, Harriet, Louisa and Daniel. Dan as he was known, unfortunately was thrown from his motorbike when a dog ran out at him. He suffered severe head injuries from which he died. This was in the year I was born. I was told incessantly that I would never have a motor-bike and it was not until my parents had died and I was in my 50s that I managed to overcome the taboo and bought a 250 Honda. Deep joy in the fundamold! (per Prof. Stanley Unwin).

My 250 Honda

Harry married Sarah Hughes and had Vera and Jack Douglass. Uncle Harry was an inveterate joker and kept us in stitches, as they say, with his tales of things that happened at work and such. He became Works Manager at Villiers Engineering, bought a house opposite the works, and asked my Dad to do the same, but he said he didn't want to live on top of his work. I remember the weekend when Uncle Harry came to show us his wage for the week—it was a five-pound note—one of the large white ones. We had never seen such wealth! Later he took over an aluminium works at Five Ways, Tipton, and Jack joined him as a pattern—maker.

Harriet married Alfred Smith and they became our parents.

Louisa married Arthur Sturgess but had no children, in later years becoming Evangelists with a mission to convert everyone in sight. I refused consistently to be converted and was a permanent disappointment to them thereby. Uncle Arthur put all his life savings into a project to convert a large villa into a church for his faith, but he was swindled out of it by a rogue solicitor who had defrauded many of his clients. He did not get any of the money back, but being a good Christian he held no malice.

As for the Smith family, only the males and Elsie married, the other girls remaining steadfastly spinsters.

James (Uncle Jim) married Mary Maria Wallace (Aunt Polly) but had no children. He was a master carpenter and built his own bungalow at Willenhall.

Alfred was our Dad. He worked as a moulder, first in Charles Lathes Ironworks and later as an aluminium caster at Villiers motorcycle works. For years he made all the gearbox covers for their bikes, but unfortunately the fumes and smoking took their toll on his lungs and his retirement was very short-lived.

George married Elsie (maiden name unknown) and had Janet.

Elsie, Dad's sister, married twice but had no children.

When we were young we walked with Dad along the canal to Bradley every Sunday morning to visit our grandparents and the aunts, who were skilled at making wine from potatoes and fruits. It was on one of these walks that we saw the Graf Zeppelin flying over, as everybody said, to take photos of possible targets. This was just before the War.

At Christmas there were big gatherings of the clans at Bradley with all sorts of Aunts, Uncles and Cousins, when party games were played—I remember particularly "Postman's Knock" which the aunts seemed to enjoy when Uncle Clarence was "The Postman". He wore those brown and white spats on his shoes—making him look quite a dandy.

Late in life, all four girls and their cousin Alice Taylor lived together and all moved into the same residential care home. All are now deceased.

So back to No. 55. This was a modest terraced house on the north side of High Street with gas lighting, a "brew-house" (utility room) and a "two-holer" toilet with buckets, emptied overnight by the "night-soil men" and a horse and cart.

There was great excitement when the time came for a little modernisation in the form of mains water, a WC, and electric light.

We lived next door to the Onions family—children Olive and Barry.

Other families in the vicinity were Ellis—their daughter called "Sister" was severely speech handicapped; Neal—their three or four sons called themselves "The black hand gang" but they were not criminals, and they eventually joined the Army in the Guards. I have no idea if they survived the War.

And of course there was "Blondie"—can't recall her name, who was "no better than she should be" in the words of my Mom and Gran. I never knew what they meant, since any reference to bedroom activity was obviously kept a total secret.

Living in a house at the rear of ours was a man called "Shed Dyer" who suffered from fits but was one of those gentle giants. One morning he was discovered standing outside in his night-shirt, weeping and rubbing his eyes with the bottom of it. Somebody asked him why he was weeping, and he replied "I'm showing my sympathy!" Ever afterwards the male genital appendage was called one's "sympathy". Who says the black—countryman has no sense of humour?

Opposite our house, on the corner of Church Lane was Marriott's shop, a typical corner shop, where lived Marge's playmate Elsie, on whose push-scooter Marge came a cropper, breaking her arm—once again calling forth arguments against the use of wheels. And again when I fell while pushing a set of pram wheels, breaking two front teeth in the process.

The area seemed to be full of Public Houses—Red Lion, Coach and Horses, George and Dragon, Rainbow. to name but a few—and something you don't see nowadays—each Pub had it's own Jazz Band playing "Kazzoos" (sounded like comb-and-paper) and drums. These bands used to parade in processions on certain occasions rather like our Gala Days and I think they marched at the time of Elections when they seemed to promote Labour rather than the Tories. My Dad always voted Liberal and got into arguments with Maggie Taylor (one of his cousins) who was absolutely Labour-mad.

I had not been inside a pub until I came home on leave in uniform and surprise surprise, my Dad asked me to go for a drink at the George & Dragon where he ran a savings club of sorts. I suppose being one of our brave boys in blue made it all right!

Came the day when we were offered a larger house— three storeys and large cellars—one of a pair of Victorian villas built by the Lones family—mine owners etc. The other one was still occupied by Arthur Lones, a bachelor who was friendly to Grandad Douglass. This was a heavenly house with long banisters for sliding down and we kids could each have our own bedroom. No. 55 must have been very crowded for the seven of us.

So into 25 Wednesbury Oak Road—still on the same main road but with a more posh road name!

The house was remarkable for the fact that although in a heavily built-up area we had an open view of fields and hills for at least two miles to the south. It got quite windy sometimes and we had to close the internal shutters on the windows—as we did also during air raids.

Looking back, Mr. Lones must have been in his seventies, and he scared us all by climbing ladders right to the roof to make repairs. Also he had an organ and at times he played it so loudly it sounded like a church. He referred to Ruby as "The little light—headed one!

No. 25 Wednesbury Oak Road

Bath-time meant a tin bath in front of the fire—there being no bathroom, but we did have an indoor toilet—water-flushed of course! There was also a small garden but not large enough to supply vegetables.

View south from No. 25.

The area abounded in derelict coalmines, and we children used to play all sorts of games among the ruins, and dangerously—down some of the (partly) filled shafts. It was like a battlefield to us but amazingly nobody got killed!

We also played the sort of games that have largely disappeared now—Whip and Top, Tipcat, Marbles, Flicking Cigarette Cards, French Cricket, Piggy-in-the-Middle, Hoop-rolling, Hop-scotch, Skipping, Leap-frog, as well as ordinary Cricket and Football.

Mom and me   *Marge, Mom and Roob*

No. 25 had an imposing front bay window until during the War a bus skidded on ice in the road, mounted the pavement and embedded itself in the bay and damaging my Mom's oak table. Again no compensation but the Bus Company had the window replaced with a common flat affair. We then offered the use of the front room as an ARP (Civil Defence) Post and a wall of sandbags was built up in front of the window, which I thought would be very useful if any bombs dropped near. In the event although ordinary bombs and parachute mines were dropped in the locality and incendiary bombs by the score, we escaped any real damage.

I was enrolled as a messenger in the ARP, patrolling on my pushbike. Also sometimes I walked round with one of the Wardens checking for chinks of light from doors or windows, because there was a total blackout to prevent enemy bombers getting any sort of target. On one occasion I was with Mr. Bryan on this duty when we came across an open front door with light showing so he knocked on the door. "Come on in," said a woman's voice. (This was about three in the morning! Mr. Bryan said "Let's get back to the Post, quick!"

I remember another occasion when I was with Mr. (Captain) Johns during an air raid—Anti-aircraft guns were blasting away merrily when a piece of shrapnel hit his steel helmet with a clang. In a flash he dropped to the ground but he wasn't hurt—he said that's what they used to do in the First World War. I said that he was more likely to get hit stretched out on the ground. We used to collect shrapnel—there were so many guns we believed it damaged more roofs than bombs did.

I did not mention that the railway ran along at the back of the house, affording opportunities for us to wave at the drivers and sometimes at passengers when main line services were diverted to "our" line following bombing problems. Also during air raids a train used to run up and down the line with a Bofors gun pooping off at any planes that came over. I'm sure, on some occasions they were also shooting at our aircraft.

One engine driver told my Dad that when he brought his goods train through Princes End at five o'clock in the morning he always blew his whistle. This woke the workers and as it was too early to get up and too late to go back to sleep the effect on population growth was considerable!!!

On the other side of the railway was the farm belonging to my Granddad's brother Dan. He was a farmer, carpenter, wheelwright, blacksmith, coffin-maker, wood-turner, welder and anything else required. His workshops were my Mecca, and I used to go to watch him work and hopefully learn a bit. He had a forge and a large gas engine for driving his machines—lathe, drills, band saw, rotary saw etc. "Remember, Boy, always keep your fingers behind the sharp bits", showing me his missing finger! Advice I still follow to the letter. I was always keen on woodwork, and fondly believed I should follow in Uncle Dan's footsteps, but the War prevented that. My mom said that I would never get married as I was married to my toolbox.

Another of my hobbies from the age of about 12 was "Wireless" or radio, as it became known. My other, young uncle Dan had been keen on this as well and had made a crystal set, the case of which I still have, and apparently the family used to listen to 2LO on headphones. I moved a little higher in the technology and made several battery-powered valve sets from instructions in the magazine "Wireless World" I have kept some of the mags. and marvel now at the way I took on the subject. There was a shop in Princes End, Jenners, I believe, where you could have your accumulators charged and you could buy all the parts necessary to make sets; baseboards, condensers (capacitors), resistors, valves, grid leaks, wire, switches, control knobs and all the other wonderful bits and pieces. Looking back, I wonder why their shop didn't go up in a big bang, because I remember they had shelves full of those accumulators, ("bottles" my Dad called them,) all merrily fizzing away, and I bet all the Jenners smoked like crazy, as did every adult in those days. I kept the skill alive, and after the War I built several sets, but this time they were mains powered, and I had a much better awareness of the dangers, following my baptism of fire with Radar sets (14 thousand volts).

I should mention also that there was a small shop opposite No. 25 where Harold Rich lived. He played the piano like a professional even at that age and he did indeed become a professional because after the War we tuned into the Pebble Mill lunchtime programme and there he was, accompanying singers etc. And he played in the Max Jaffa Trio.

The area was criss-crossed with canals and we were always told to keep away from the "cut". There was a lot of traffic on them up to and during the war, mainly horse-drawn. In the winter, when the water froze an icebreaker was used to clear a path. This was a barge with a flat deck and a handrail along the middle. About twenty men used to stand alongside the rail and rock the boat furiously from side to side while the poor horse(s) struggled to pull it along, thereby cracking the ice. In the summer we kids used to get on this barge and pretend we were breaking the ice (until driven away by the boatmen).

But I am getting ahead of myself. Our schooldays started at Princes End Joint School—Infants and then

Junior—Headmaster Mr. Turley. Strangely I don't remember much about events at that school except that a horrible big dentist named Mr. Titmus ripped out three of my teeth and obviously started a life-long hatred of the profession.

Time to move to senior school—Marge went to Bilston Girls High School. Ruby and I both went to Tipton Selective Central School, (now apparently called Alexandra High School)—both good schools; and we are ever grateful for the education we received at our respective establishments. As far as my school was concerned, the emphasis was more on the idea that you should learn *how* to learn, rather than cram a lot of facts that may or may not be of any use.

There is much argument these days about metrication taking over from imperial measurements but as I tell the present day youngsters, we were taught to use both systems, so could take up whichever was suitable for the matter in hand.

The Masters at my School were:

Ralph Bassett—Music

Harry Lamb—French

"Bonzo" Brookes—Geography

"Bags" Bailey—Maths.

Mr. Cooper—History

"Tich" Woodcroft—English

Mr. Lane—Commerce

Mr. Whitcroft—Art. (He had a steel plate in his head from a wartime injury).

Timothy Bolus—Science

Mr. Butler—Woodwork

Grumpy" Gilbert—Metalwork. Replaced later by Mr. Pitney

Mr. Hancock—PT (Now called Physical Ed.")

My prowess in the sports arena was not very spectacular although I did learn to play badminton, practised putting on the grassed quadrangle, and once ran in a mile race (and I'm still out of breath from it). And I also obtained my dislike of swimming after being thrown into the swimming bath without any warning by the aforesaid

Hancock. He once rode his motorbike between two other bikes at night but they turned out to be the rear lights on a lorry! We did laugh!

It was during a maths lesson when Mr. Bailey called me out to the front of the class because I could not see what he was getting at on the board so a little humiliation was required. Both he and I hadn't realised was that literally I couldn't see it—not that I couldn't understand it. Off then quickly to Headmaster Mr. Graham's study to check with a sightchart and everyone realised I was short-sighted. There followed visits to Wolverhampton Eye Infirmary where I was given spectacles. The first time I went outside wearing them I was totally amazed at how clear everything was. I could even read posters across the street. It had never occurred to me that eyesight could be any different to the way I saw things. From then on I enjoyed maths. and didn't get any more caning for being thick at the subject!

We had some good trips from School—once to London when we visited the Science Museum—saw our first television set working—then to The Palladium to see the Crazy Gang, followed by a meal at Lyons Corner House where we were served by "Nippies" in their uniforms, a great day out for Midlanders.

On another occasion we had a coach trip to Carding Mill Valley out Ludlow way—that was the first time I had seen real country with hills and we actually climbed up the said hills—magical!

Carding Mill Valley

Mr. Bassett formed a school orchestra and I was volunteered to take up the violin goodness—how everybody suffered while I practised—but fortunately the house was large enough for me to get some distance away. Marge was learning to play the piano and eventually I could play well enough for us to play duets. Also one Sunday our orchestra was sent to Dudley Parish Church to play Haydn's Creation with the choir and organ. One member of the orchestra—Jones—went on to a long career with the Birmingham

Symphony—when he was with us he made us sound like rubbish.

It was about this time when I became interested in aircraft and even gave "lectures" at school on various aspects of flying, although I knew my eyesight would make it very difficult for me to become a pilot.

Academically I think I did quite well—in the Oxford Junior Exam (equivalent to O levels) I had eight successes, while in the Oxford School Certificate (equivalent to A levels) I achieved nine. I also obtained a UEI Certificate in Engineering Science. Eventually I finished up as a Senior Prefect. One of my classmates Ken Devall who was very good at Maths became a Navigator in the RAF, force landed in Spain, escaped to Gibraltar and while flying back to England in a Sunderland was shot down over the Atlantic. He was just one of the many school friends who did not survive the War.

While on the subject of schooldays I must mention that I contracted Bell's Paralysis in 1938 (the facial paralysis) and Dr. Murdoch told me to go to Wolverhampton Hospital three times a week for treatment. In my ignorance I took this to mean that I should not go to school, so for three months I was at home and doing the visits. The Hospital then said I should sign off at the doctor's and when I said to him "I suppose this means I have to go back to school now" he nearly had a fit and said "You shouldn't have been off school all that time". It was a wonderful Summer!

The school motto was "Loyalty", and what I can remember of the school song is an appendix at the end of this opus.

I left school in 1939 just in time for the start of WW2 and in accordance with the regulations I was sent to work in a drawing office at Wrights Forge & Engineering at

Tipton where I was trained as a draughtsman. I worked on various Admiralty projects, such as de-gaussing apparatus for ships, anti-mine equipment, mobile harbours for use in the D-Day landings, as well as other normal things like steel buildings, gas producers and equipment for rubber factories (before Malaya was lost to the Japs).

Our boiler shop produced large welded and riveted tanks—the noise they made was horrendous. They also produced pre-fabricated tugs in three pieces to be welded together later. There was great consternation when the first set was completed—no-one had thought how to get them out of the building to load them on to three low-loaders for the long journey to the coast!

Removing the whole end of the workshop and altering it so that it could be removed again for the next lot solved the problem.

Besides drawing I was also the "chief photo-printer" operating a massive machine with carbon-arc lamps to make blueprints with ferro-prussiate paper and brown-and-white prints with ferro-gallic paper. These then had to be developed in a large zinc tray and hung up to dry. This experience stood me in good stead later on in the Far East when I was able to make a sort of solar photo-printer to save a lot of copying work.

And being the latest addition to the staff I was also given the job of "chief chemist" testing the feedwater for the huge boilers that provided steam for the hammers in the forge shop. This meant using various acids, methyl orange, amyl acetate and so on to check the pH value of the water, which apparently was vital for the health of the boilers.

The work was deemed a reserved occupation and so not liable to conscription but two of us wanted to get into the RAF—Duncan Preston and myself. As far as I know we were the only two to see active service out of the nine in that office.

At this time I joined the ATC—No.240 Wednesbury Squadron and eventually became Cadet Flight Sergeant, giving lectures in various subjects. I was waiting to join the RAF as a Radar Navigator—(they accepted chaps with glasses for that at that time) Later they had enough recruits so I didn't get to do much in that line although I had the training for it. Perhaps it was as well because the Beaufighters being used for night fighters were notorious for suddenly dropping like a brick on approaching the airfield. Far too high a wingloading for comfort. My RAFVR number during that time was 1583190. "Discharged as surplus to requirements".

Beaufighter   *Lancaster*

Objects of Desire!

So with that door closed I tried another tack, applying to join the ATA (Air Transport Auxiliary) ferry pilots organisation. This I thought would be pure flying—no guns, no radios, just ferrying planes from factories or from one base to another. Quite a few of the aristocratic ladies were already flying, because they had had pilot's licences (and their own planes) before the War. However, I was accepted for flying training until they discovered I was under 19 years of age and therefore not allowed. (At that time some of my friends were already flying bombers over Germany, albeit under 19). The upshot was that they told me to come back after my 19th birthday.

Well that I did, only to be told that now the RAF had a surplus of trained pilots and they were being transferred to the ATA. Another door slammed in my face.

All this time I had been badgering Group Capt. Wright at the RAF Recruiting Centre in Birmingham and he finally said "Why not go in on the Ground Staff and I will put a word in for you to do flying training?"

By this time I was a little disillusioned with the whole business so I agreed to go on the Ground Staff. He could offer me Link Trainer Instructor or Draughtsman so I chose the easier of the two, since I was already trained.

While waiting for the call to enlist again, Duncan and I took a holiday in Scotland, by taking our bikes on the train to Glasgow; staying overnight with his Aunt Galbraith and cousin Mona before cycling all the way over Rest-and-be—Thankful (a mountain) and down into the Mull of Kintyre to Craigie Castle estate at Tayinloan where his relatives lived—Mr. Reid being the head keeper. This was a great adventure for me as I had never seen real mountains and lochs before. Duncan was a bird-watcher so we spent long hours walking along beaches and up in the hills spotting all sorts of birds I had never even heard of. The sound of the Curlew call still brings back memories. On one occasion we were on a beach when a squadron of Swordfish planes came diving down at us and we realised we were in the middle of a practise firing range. Fortunately the Wren observers in a spotting tower must have seen us because the planes turned away. We moved away very quickly!

Largie Castle   *Mona and Mrs.Galbraith*

During our time there Duncan caught a chill out fishing in a boat on a loch—(I did the rowing) and it seemed to be turning to pneumonia, so our 10 day holiday stretched to 3 weeks—much to the annoyance of our Welsh chief draughtsman back at home. All turned out well, however and we came back safe and sound. On the journey north, being lads in "civvies" we had pretended to be merchant seamen on the way to join our ship in Scotland because there was a lot of "aggro" towards men people thought should be in the Services.

While I waited to go into the RAF several of my friends were lost—Ken Devall I mentioned before, Jack Key killed crashing into a mountain in Wales, George Boffy killed in a Swordfish attacking a German battleship and Tom Allaway shot down flying in a Wellington over Germany.

(While I was writing this a strange coincidence happened. I saw the name of Tom's sister Lily on the Net, and I have since been in touch with her and her husband Roy by Email at their home in British Columbia, Canada).

So on June 8th two days after the D-Day invasion of Normandy I responded to the call of King and

Douglas Smith

Country and reported to Cardington to be enrolled in His Majesty's Royal Air Force for the second time as 3061061 AC2 Smith A.D.

Thence to West Drayton for a trade test and finally given the Trade of Draughtsman Group 1.

From there to Arbroath on the East Coast of Scotland for introduction to drill etc. (remember I had been doing that as an instructor in the ATC for some years)

While there I learned how to peel a ton of potatoes, to strip and rebuild a machine gun, fire a Sten gun and a 303 rifle, bayonet a straw bale, throw a hand grenade and stand sentry watch at the Quay side in case there was an invasion. I had twin Vickers guns mounted on a stand and a sealed box of alleged ammunition. A boat came in without lights about two o'clock in the morning, and while I was wondering what to do about it a Scottish voice shouted out—thank goodness it was a fishing boat.

Grenade throwing practise took place at a quarry. Two "erks" and a corporal stood behind a wall of sandbags on the edge and hurled their grenades at a target on the floor of the quarry and watched to see I if the aim was good before they exploded, ducking down when the corporal said "DOWN". I was there with one AC2 Pocock who threw his "black pineapple" straight up in the air and it came down and landed smoking on top of the sandbags. The corporal calmly pushed it over the edge of the wall where it exploded. By this time the said Pocock was flat on his face on the ground and the officer up in the observation tower said, "Give that man a clean pair of trousers, Corporal!"

The locals and holidaymakers had a great time laughing at us as we screamed and launched ourselves at the straw figures with our fixed bayonets. However we lived through the course and got unprecedented praise from the W.O. in charge when we performed like guardsmen at our passing-out parade.

Then I was promoted to AC1 and sent to 60 Group HQ in a big house near Leighton Buzzard. It may have been Mentmore but I never got to know that because there was an absolute regime of secrecy. The "raison d'etre" of the place was to evaluate and apply new radar apparatus for use in operations from ideas thrown up by the boffins at TRE Malvern (in full the Telecommunications Research Establishment), brainchild of Professor Watson-Watt.

There I learned the art of drawing plotting maps, engraving PPI masks (for the front of Radar screens) circuit diagrams of immense complication, detailed drawings of modifications to Radar apparatus and copies of peculiar Radar coverage diagram, (Echo Charts).

Having been given the works I was then posted to SEAAF to do the same work out there—South East Asia Air Forces. So off to Liverpool to embark on the "Orontes" then to Greenock to join a large convoy through the Bay of Biscay, Mediterranean, Suez Canal, Aden and on to Bombay.

ORIENT LINE S.S. "ORONTES." 20,000 TONS

SS Orontes

On the journey we were escorted by Destroyers—forever dashing round dropping depth charges—the noise of these made a clang on the ship's side like a hammer blow. One can only imagine what it must have been like for the crew of submarines. Through the Med. dolphins also escorted us and we were amazed at the clarity of the deep blue water. There were also large shoals of multicoloured jellyfish. Passing through the Suez Canal was also memorable—the navigation in the narrow channel was very skilful, but of course it was one way at a time.

For some reason that we were not told we stopped in the harbour at Aden for some days, with a yellow flag flying (quarantine), and the heat was tremendous when the ship was stationary. It was very good to get under way again. Eventually we reached Bombay.

After a stay in a Transit Camp outside Bombay, where we were introduced to the horrors of Indian toilet facilities, a troop train took us to Calcutta—then a ferry journey and another train (narrow gauge) to Chittagong—10 days in all. We had to survive on "K rations"—mostly dried food that had to be re-constituted, and soup or tea made with hot water from the engine whenever we stopped.

At times we were shunted into a siding perhaps for several hours in order not to upset the normal train services, when we could take the opportunity of an unofficial shower under the water towers that supplied the engines.

Sleeping on the train was a hit and miss affair—some slept on the floor, some on the seats and I chose to tie myself onto the luggage rack. A bit of a mistake really because it was the monsoon season, the roof leaked and I had to sleep with a towel over me to catch the rainwater.

In the daytime a favourite pastime was to sit on the step in the doorway to get some breeze, but it was scary when we went over one of those skeletal river bridges and there was literally nothing below your feet.

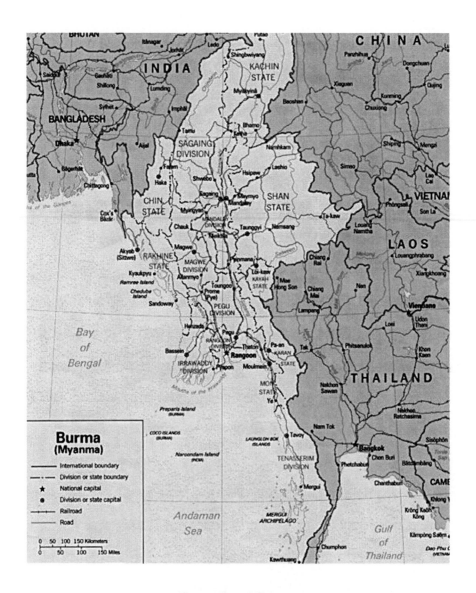

Bengal and Burma

In Chittagong I was taken to HQ 182 Wing which was the controlling station for all Radar operations in Bengal and Burma. I was surprised to find that I was the only RAF draughtsman in that theatre of war. They had been relying on getting anybody who knew the right end of a pencil to attempt quite complicated problems. When I told them I had been sent from 60 Group they thought all their birthdays had come at once and I was rapidly given a thorough briefing on the jobs to be done. A total of about 37 Radar Stations (many mobile in amphibious DUKWS or large vehicles) had to be serviced with plotting maps, PPI masks, Perspex range scales, the usual modification drawings and goodness knows what else.

We had a good set of workshops, which could turn out anything from a solar photo-printing device for blueprints to aerial towers or repairs to sets (because it was almost impossible to get anything official sent out from UK). I even wrote to my Mom and asked her to send me my proper drawing instruments, which she did, because up to then they had only had schoolboy tools.

Jimmy Hill   *Bill Palmer, Frank Gaines Ron Fleckney*

We even made a "Heath Robinson" affair to mould Perspex into the shape required to fit over the front of the radar screens because we could not get blanks sent out from UK. Fill a tube (like a TV tube) with concrete; suspend it over another concrete mould with a depression matching the tube. Insert electric heating wires, fill the depression with water, allow to heat up, place the flat blank on the surface and let the weight of the top bit press the blank into the required shape. These were called PPI masks. Necessity, they say . . . . I engraved the necessary grid and coastline on the masks before they were moulded.

The "domestic" site consisted of a bungalow commandeered from the local railway boss Mr. Greatorex and a series of bamboo "bashas" (huts) situated a mile from the technical site in virgin jungle. It was *HOT,* and drawing maps on linen was an absolute pain because of the perspiration which tended to drip on them. I found myself having to work until midnight every day to keep up with the demand for maps and other things, owing to the rapid movement forward of the Mobiles. So I recruited some Radar Mechanics from our "spare pool" if they had any clue at all about drawing or photo-printing.

One of them was Brian A. White, who was a great "word-smith", and he penned a poem about me and my doings at 182. This is also in an appendix at the end. On one occasion General Slim came to look round and when he went into the workshops one of the bods was frying some bacon and eggs on a burner. Without batting an eyelid he sat down and asked if he could join in. He was a great guy—universally liked, which is more than could be said for the Supremo Mountbatten.

As the war was still well and truly on, work carried on seven days a week and in my case mostly from 8am to midnight. One Sunday morning I was walking to the office with two members of the Orderly Room staff when we were stopped by an officious RAF policeman (fresh out from Blighty) and challenged because we were "5 minutes late". The poor soul did not realise he was talking to the Sergeant in charge of postings so within 24 hours he was on his way to a forward area to exercise his authority!

A Jap recce. aircraft used to fly over every morning, but we always ignored it so that they could not identify our anti-aircraft gun sites. And we were not very pleased when American bomber crews going off on missions tested their guns by firing at our Radar stations— fortunately they did not seem to be accurate shooters! There were tigers in the hills round about, and one was a man-eater we were told, but we never saw any signs, thank goodness.

Very large spiders were more of a threat, especially in the shower.

One lad was bitten on the leg by one of them—his leg swelled up like a balloon, he was taken away and we never saw him again. Another problem for some bods was that they could not perspire. This was treated as a serious matter and they were immediately sent back to Blighty

The CO of 182 was Wing Commander Strutt, and my bosses in the office were Flt. Lt. Margolis, who knew what he was doing and W/O Budden who wandered around in a sort of daze—I never heard him say anything remotely connected with the job.

Mr. Margolis was very keen to keep the staff up to date with developments in Radar and to this end he used to issue what he called "Palm-side Chats". A common joke was to ask any "green" new boys to shin up the aerial and polish the lobes—(the invisible radiation put out from the antenna). (Well, you had to have a sense of humour to remain sane out there!)

An unfortunate incident occurred when an American bomber returning from a long mission passed through our airspace heading for Calcutta on a pitch-black night without operating their IFF to identify the plane as friendly. As it could have been a large Jap Bomber we sent up 2 Beaufighters to intercept. They could not identify it so they were ordered to shoot it down. The crew baled out but were picked up by our air-sea rescue boats, They were very grateful until they learned we had shot them down—they thought the plane had caught fire. Relations were somewhat strained between the USAF and RAF for a while! I have always believed it was a Superfort but in a book about the Beaufighter it was claimed to be a B17 Flying Fortress, and that some of the crew died.

As the Japs were being pushed further south towards Singapore our Radar stations kept moving forward, past Cox's Bazaar, Akyab, Kyaukpu, Ramree, Sandoway and towards Rangoon, until it was decided we were no longer needed. So we were withdrawn across the River Brahmaputra on a top-heavy ferry and way back to Belgaum south of Poona. Here we were re-formed into 2BS&RU (Base Signals and Radar Unit) preparing to invade Singapore.

Nanga Parbat
from Gulmarg

We had not had any leave, so while the Unit was being formed, Jimmy Hill (no, not that one!), Malcolm Tinning and I decided to go for a break to Kashmir. This was like deciding to go to Moscow from here! However the powers that be allowed us to go for a month, gave us first class travel to Srinagar and further into the Himalayas. I can only say that no holiday can ever top that one—of course this was before India and Pakistan started getting stupid about ownership of Kashmir The views were unbelievable—we could see Kanchenjunga (?) 80 miles away and it still looked way up high in the sky, and at night we saw lightning flashing over the distant peaks. Indescribable.

The Ganderbal Hills

Part of that trip included a day-long journey by gharry (lorry) from the foot-hills up mad winding roads up to Srinagar ("Look Sahib says the Indian Army driver, taking his eyes off the road—down there gharry went last week"), only at the time we were looking down on clouds! We also went up much higher to Gulmarg, a sort of winter sports place at about 12,000 feet. Here we were accommodated in wooden cabins with fireplaces but there was a main building—a Hotel with golf course etc.

The year after we went there some RAF bods were sent up there in Winter as a survival exercise but the Hotel burnt down and they really had to survive in tents dropped by air. There were no roads up to that place— everyone either walked or rode on ponies, and that was not possible through the snowdrifts in winter.

From Srinagar I posted home some silk underwear (ladies), some silk scarves and a carved wooden lamp. I still have the last two items, but not the first!

It was a good break but then we had to go back down those scary roads and on to the railway and thence back to Belgaum. There we found everybody desperately trying to sort out the new unit which was housed in about 120 vehicles—being totally mobile.

I was given a 3-ton lorry fitted out as a drawing office but because I did not drive they allocated me a driver—Ron Fleckney, a wonderfully witty Londoner. The vehicles included offices, kitchens, workshops, electrical generators, repair and rescue, water carriers, Officers Jeeps, in fact we were literally a mobile town. And all this lot had to be driven across India in a huge convoy to somewhere near Madras to await loading on to landing craft and then hopefully off-loaded on to the beach at Singapore, no doubt with a warm welcome from the Japs who were still in occupation. So we waited a few days and then we were called on parade, ostensibly to be given our final instructions before embarking.

Instead we were told that a large bomb had been dropped on Japan and the Japs had decided to surrender, consequently we would not be needed to cover the invasion. Our vehicles would be sent on but the personnel would follow in a troopship. Joy (as they say) was unconfined. The thought of running up a beach armed with a tee-square and possibly a Sten in the face of angry Japs had not been one's best idea for a day at the seaside.

So we waited until a ship came to pick us up—no landing craft this, but the "SS Esperance Bay". On board were us technical bods and a party of WRNS, ATS and Nurses. A troopship had never been like that—shoes polished, faces shaved, language modified to the point of normal polite conversation and everybody on their best behaviour. The girls were given the privilege of going up to the top deck with the Officers, but only one did so—a rather snooty Wren. The rest of us stayed on the lower deck during the day, passing the time pleasantly enough playing cards and fetching endless cups of tea or coffee. I didn't see or hear of any activity that you couldn't tell your Mom about, apart from "her up there" and we were at Singapore all too soon.

SS Esperance Bay

(On the way we went through the Malacca Straits when the Captain said, "If you look to port you will see seven waterspouts". When we asked "Are they dangerous?" he said "Only if they hit us!"

After disembarkation we were taken to Paya Lebar to the east of the city, where we were housed in a bicycle factory and it's workers' houses. Our vehicles were already parked on the airstrip, which was a satellite of Changi Airfield. The workshops had a good range of machine tools and also included a raised drawing office looking over the shop floor that became my domain. I transferred my equipment from my lorry to the office and after that I didn't see it again. (Aaaaaaaah, bless it!)

In my office at Paya Lebar

My Drawing Office Lorry parked at Paya Lebar

2 BS & RU Workshops Crew

Douglas Smith

That's me on the left in pale tunic and Bush Hat!.

My work was somewhat different from 182 Wing in that there were no enemy aircraft to track and clobber, so no need for the plotting maps and things, except when an Exhibition was laid on in Singapore to show how we had coped with the problems. I now had a new boss—Flt. Lt. "Joe" Blake who was an excellent Technical Officer and very approachable. While the exhibition was on who should arrive to look round but my old boss from 182— Flt. Lt. Margolis.

"Hello Smith", he said, "I thought I detected your handiwork, but what happened, those maps were not as good as we had at Sambre". "Oh well", said I, "there isn't the same desperation here, and I don't think the locals would be any the wiser".

I had to design and produce some heavy engineering in the shape of searchlight towers to oversee the airstrip and entry barriers for the site entrance. Also a Radar building to be erected on the top of Changi Airfield Control Tower.

A detachment from TRE was sent to work on our station dreaming up all sorts of ideas, as was their wont—typical Boffins. They came up with a system called Loran—Babs which was to guide pilots flying to Ceylon, Hong Kong or Northern Australia. This saved them from having to navigate by the normal means and merely meant they followed radio beams like landing systems. The actual apparatus had to be made up from any equipment we could make or cannibalise. So the mechanical means of switching the beams was another Heath Robinson affair, consisting of motors, reduction gears from Jap aircraft dumped on our airstrip, hack-saw blades for spring contacts and cams formed from Tufnol

in our own workshop.

That was in 1945/6 and to my surprise,

59

when I went to work in 1950 at Chichester Rural District Council, one of the chaps in my office, Frank Hotston, had been stationed in Singapore and had tales about this strange clanking mechanism that was still going strong! Small world!

One morning Mr. Blake came into my office and said he had been made up to Sqn. Ldr. I congratulated him and said that I could use some stripes as well, being then only LAC. He asked how to do it and I told him he would need to give me a trade test. He said that I should organise one and he would do the rest. So I produced some sort of complicated drawing exercise (which he sent to wherever it had to go) and lo-and-behold up came my promotion to Corporal in Station Orders!

It was not all work now that the war was over—time was made for various pursuits like badminton, cricket and football—see the picture of a comic football match at Christmas 1945—Officers and Other Ranks had a hilarious game partly due to the alcoholic haze!

There were several amusement parks in the city, with names like "Happy World", where it was possible to eat, buy souvenirs and dance in the Malayan style—no physical contact you understand. On one occasion, after we had been dropped off by the duty wagon, the driver couldn't start the engine again to go back. We found that some crafty native had removed the battery while we were disembarking! Another incident occurred when one night somebody removed the wheels from all our Jeeps on the airstrip in spite of having searchlights playing from the towers all night.

Good luck ran out when Joe B. was posted and his replacement—one Flt. Lt. Hodgson took over as Technical Officer. What a disaster that was—he was totally ignorant of all matters engineering-wise—we thought that as a technical officer he made a good milkman. I had several arguments with him on various mathematical and scientific problems, but he would not listen to any advice that we, the engineering front line had to offer. We had several Malayans who had been members of the STC, (Special Technical Corps), very skilled in things like lathe work, welding etc. Hodgson told one of them to turn a quarter of an inch off the diameter of a *rubber* roller for a typewriter he had "acquired". The poor chap came to ask me what to do, almost in tears, so I told him to do it as Hodgson had said, by feeding the tool in the full quarter inch at once, and of course, rubber being rubber it completely chewed it up. I told H. that it would only have been possible if we had some liquid nitrogen to solidify the rubber but we did not. He was not best pleased and the situation deteriorated to the point where he even accused me of taking "his" transport when I requested a Jeep to go on a surveying trip, in spite of the driver confirming that he had come for me.

His only contribution to our work was to ask for a house-load of teak furniture to be made in our woodwork shop so it could be crated up and shipped to England as "technical equipment" for his own use. I had two Indians helping me in the drawing office— one, C.S.Doshi also ran an export/import business in the city and one day he asked me if I would stay in Singapore after demob. and have my name on his letter heading. It was tempting; but fate intervened when I was struck down with appendicitis, rushed across the island to Seletar on a very bumpy road and duly had the offending bit removed. From the hospital I was put on a train with a crowd of walking wounded across the Johore Causeway to a convalescent Centre in the Cameron Highlands. It was like Scotland but with jungle surrounding it.

The native Nagas who lived in the jungle were fiercely pro-British as a result of the efforts of pre-war District Commissioners, and during the war they created havoc with the Japs who stupidly attacked their villages. They were deadly accurate with blow-pipes.

While I was there two of them came running to the hospital to say they had found two of our nurses who had gone walking in the jungle and lost their way. They would not approach the girls but showed one of the Staff were they had got to.

After about a week there, I was told to report to the docks at Singapore asap, because my name had been drawn out of the hat for a month's leave in Blighty, one of only 120 bods so chosen.

SS Mooltan

My unit were not told about this—they thought I had gone to that great Radar Station in the sky! However I joined the ship, the "SS Mooltan" and had a pleasant trip back to dear old England. Had a thoroughly good time basking in the glory of being one of our brave boys who beat the Japs. And the month extended to two months due to the lack of ships to go back.

When I was eventually recalled we were embarked on the "SS Samaria", which only went to Bombay. We assumed that the travel people thought Singapore was just down the road a bit. We were dumped in that Transit Camp again because they said "We don't have any ships going from here to Singapore".

CUNARD WHITE STAR S.S. "SAMARIA."

SS Samaria

Then they told us we would go to Calcutta and take ship from there. By train again across to Calcutta (several days), then into a Transit Camp there. We were told that no ships were expected, especially as the Hindu/Muslim riots were getting out of hand. So they sent us out on the streets armed with Stens to try to keep the peace. Impossible—there were bodies on the streets and many were thrown into the river. Horrible.

Eventually they sent us down to Vizagapatam, way down the east coast towards Madras, again to hang about in a camp, doing nothing, for a fortnight or so.

Suddenly we were paraded to be told that a hospital ship with engine trouble was calling and going on to Singapore and would we be ready to jump aboard the "Dunera".

SS Dunera

A pleasant journey followed, although we were hoping that the engines would keep going! They did and we disembarked at Singapore six months after I had been taken to Seletar—only to be dumped yet again in a transit camp about a fourpenny tram ride from my base at Paya Lebar. But would you believe I was not allowed to leave the camp "until the proper paperwork arrived".

They let us out eventually and when I got back to 2BS&RU my colleagues were surprised. Bob Avery who was in my billet said "We thought you had died when we found you were not at the Cameron Highlands. Oh, and then by-the-way you were made up to Sergeant for a time but they gave you up for lost and brought in somebody else to do your job." This was the last straw and it was only a few weeks before I was on my way again back to Blighty.

This time the ship was the Queen of Bermuda, a very grand old lady in normal times, but rather crowded with the number of people being repatriated. I note that we sailed from Singapore on March 19th. 1947, and docked in Liverpool on the 15th April. That was the sixth voyage to and from the Far East and I often said I probably spent more time on ships than many Navy bods did!

Q.T.E.V. "QUEEN OF BERMUDA" AT PORT SAID.

SS Queen of Bermuda

That proved to be my last troopship voyage and when I landed I was posted to Old Sarum where I was to be the Chief Draughtsman in the School of Land/Air Warfare. This was another completely different change of occupation. The School was run for bigwigs like the top brass of all the Services, ostensibly to teach them the skills of co-operation in matters military. Our task was to provide visual aids for lectures—huge charts showing chains of command, backdrops and other stage effects for playlets, apart from the more mundane things like place-cards for dinners, maps of the camp etc. Also I had to make a copy of the Station Crest for use on stationery etc.

School of Land/Air Warfare, Old Sarum

Here I learned how to paint scenery and produce large printed charts with one-stroke brushes.—and once again time was pressing—an Officer would come in the afternoon with a draft plan or something and say that it was wanted for say "10 o'clock in the morning". Oh joy, another late night job! This could be a piece probably twelve feet by eight.

Demonstrations were given, including mass parachute drops on the airfield, and on one such the assembled audience of Officers had the horrific sight of a paratrooper plummeting down to crash right in front of them when his chute failed to open. I was about 200 yards away but I can still remember his screaming all the way down.

I was billeted in one of the airmen's huts with one Eddie Clapham, a regular Bod, a photographer in charge of the photo equipment used to demonstrate the uses of photography in the field. He was one of the great witty characters one found in the RAF those days, much prone to riding a bike like it was a horse, and on the lookout for opportunities to use the equipment for a little gain, (Just to keep it in good working order, you understand!). He had a lucrative idea to take photos of all the participants at the Station Sports Day, rush to get prints, and put them on show at the evening dance, to catch all the athletes in a good mood and take orders for proper prints. He lent me one of his Leicas so that the two of us could be taking photos all afternoon. I don't know if he made any profit.

When he married his Barbara I had to stand in as his Best Man because his friend who was supposed to do it had gone off on the Queen Mary to be an official cruise photographer. What a day—"Hunnaccustomed as I ham to public speaking etc."

Well, at this time I became aware of a WAAF by the name of Joan Gamble, Station Hairdresser, who consented to become my lady wife.

The rest is more than 50 years of married bliss, but that is quite another story!

After demob. I returned to No. 25 and went to work for Staffordshire County Council Planning Dept. first at Park Hall, a magnificent Country Mansion and later at another smaller house Ellerslie, in Riley Crescent in Goldthorn Hill.

Here we ran the Area Planning Office for the southern area of Staffordshire, under Mr. H.G. Avery, dealing with day—to—day planning applications and preparing zoning maps for the various towns and villages. Other colleagues were Mr. Alford, H. Green, W. Cartwright, Neville Aston, Powell, Freda Round, Barbara ???? and another typist whose name escapes me.

Southern Area Planning Office, Wolverhampton

Mr. Green had been in the Army in Burma

at the time of the Jap invasion and had led his troops on the long march back to India when they could no longer stop the enemy advance. At the first Army Base they reached in India he was told off for being badly dressed for an Army Officer—this from people who never knew what the jungle looked like!

Neville Aston was a dear friend who sadly died from Diabetes a few years later while working on the Isle of Wight.

Freda Round was the niece of Dorothy Round, a pre-war Wimbledon tennis player, when they wore those long white dresses.

We were married on August 13 at Christ Church, Coseley, the same church where my parents had been married, and lived for a time at No. 25 with them and Ruby, who had married Howard (Pete) Weston. Marge had also married (Norman Weston), Pete's brother and had moved away.

After a time I applied for, and obtained a position with Chichester Rural District Council as a planning assistant. At my interview I produced one of the maps I had drawn for the future development of a village in our area in the Midlands. This map included provision for three Churches—how was I to know that the Chairman of the Council present at the interview was Rev. Hearn?

The Council provided us with a house, 15 Highfield Lane, Oving and what do you think, that lovely man the Rev. Hearn was the Vicar. He and his wife were the epitome of kindness, just as one imagined a rural Vicar and his wife. They used to visit people and take baskets of eggs or fruit to anyone ill or in dire straits. For a time I became a Church Warden alongside John Walker, the village school headmaster and Mr. Hearn used to invite us round to the Rectory for a cup of tea or whatever.

Years later the then Clerk of the Council, G.T.Giles said "Mr. Smith, that was a very shrewd move to show Mr. Hearn that map with the Churches".

It meant that the favourite for the job (an existing employee) didn't stand a chance. The loser never let me forget it.

Oving was alongside Tangmere RAF Station and we had a great time seeing the planes take off and land. We had Mosquitoes, Meteors, Vampires, Lightnings, Hunters, Canberras, Andovers, Hercules, Shackletons to name but

a few. The open days on the airfield were very exciting because where we lived was right under where the flying action took place although somewhat scary at times.

Our little Rosalind was born at home at No. 15 and to say she was born to know aircraft is a veritable truth, as a Squadron of fighters took off right over the house at the time. No wonder she wound up at the Royal Aeronautical Society (RAeS) in London later on!

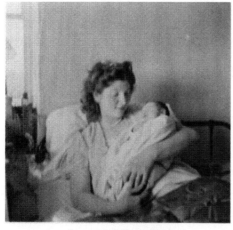

Joan and Rosalind

I worked in Planning and Building Regulations there from July 1950 to January 1982, finishing up as Senior Admin. Officer for the enlarged Chichester District Council when Chichester City, Petworth Rural, and Midhurst Rural Districts were combined with Chi. Rural District.

In December 1963 we moved to No. 7 Church Lane Tangmere, into one of the houses built to accommodate staff when the requisitioned Tangmere Rectory was demolished to make way for the future Hearn Close development. At the time all 6 houses were occupied by staff, but after a few years only 2 remain occupied by ex-staff. Five have now been bought by the residents.

At that time Ernie Elson, who also designed many private houses in the posh parts of Middleton, near Bognor Regis, designed the Council houses. He was quite a character, having been a pilot flying Avro 504s with (Sir) Alan Cobham's Air Circus before the War. They gave five-shilling flights from any available large field, and I remember one such near the Wolverhampton to Birmingham main road. Their home base then was next to what became Ford airfield during the War, but then Sir Alan moved to Dorset to develop refuelling in flight which is now commonplace in all Air Forces.

My main job was to write planning reports to present to Committees dealing with planning applications, carry out Land Charges Searches but also to visit sites for development, check public footpaths for obstructions or dumped litter, and discuss proposals with developers. I was also required to attend Public Enquiries on appeals, to present the Council's case, and to give evidence in Court cases at Chichester or the High Court in London.

I was glad to be able to retire in January 1982 because we were beginning to get recruits from universities whose technical knowledge was impeccable, but whose skill at dealing with long—established builders and developers was sadly lacking in tact or courtesy. Any builder who did not know, say, the pH value of his concrete or the modulus of elasticity of his steel beams was considered a moron by two of these over-inflated egos, and they had the same feelings about all the other officers and Councillors. Not a good way to become flavour of the month! Fortunately both of them went their ways—one to South Africa, (pity the poor blacks!).

So I left the office without a backward glance as they say. And I have never regretted it.

AMEN

And in November that year our Grandson "Hammi" was born, bless him! That would start another story!

Camping Days

From the late 1950s we took to camping, after we acquired our first car, a dear little Austin 7 Ruby (1938 vintage). No heater, manual windscreen wiper, semaphore direction indicators.

Austin 7 Ruby 1938

Our first trip was to a campsite at Brighton, when it rained of course, and our tents were not very waterproof. But it was a great adventure and an introduction to some of the friendliest people on

Earth. We soon splashed out on a "proper" tent, a blue Cabanon frame tent—what luxury! Separate bedrooms, and an area for cooking. A small trailer made packing easier. We were invited to join a "meet" one weekend with the Camping Club, by our friends John and Gwynneth Harris, and we were so taken into the fold as it were, that we decided to join the Club. In 1968 we changed to a touring caravan, a Sprite Alpine 12 footer, and continued until about 1980, when it was becoming a little too much.

Camping in the New Forest

That was the start of many happy years when we camped almost every weekend with the West Sussex District Association in various places throughout Sussex and Kent. This was mainly on farms or sometimes in fields attached to a pub, and our aim was to leave the site looking as though we had not been there, to the extent of "combing" the grass. This worked so well that once a farmer phoned the secretary and asked why we had not used his field!

We spent holidays as well, camping in the New Forest, Devon and Cornwall, Wales and Scotland.

After getting the caravan we usually took three weeks holiday at a time, in order to reach northern Scotland, which we could do in two days and then with a two day journey back home. That left us sufficient time to see the Highlands and Islands properly. Over the years there was no part of Scotland we did not visit, and we loved it.

We had some quite remarkable times north of the Border; our first camp site at Kinlochewe gave us our first taste of a storm Force 10, causing us to tie the van down to the car. And on one occasion, driving along the side of Loch Lomond the gear lever came off in my hand, causing no little consternation, a problem that was solved by an AA man fetching a piece of exhaust pipe from a garage and jamming it over the stub. Our temper was not improved before the AA man arrived when an Indian car driver behind berated us for "parking in that stupid spot". This happened on Saturday morning and fortunately we were able to get to a Vauxhall garage in Glasgow before they closed, and get it repaired.

And of course there was the year when we spent three weeks up there and it rained every day until the day we started back home, when we got sunburnt in the car. But the rainbows were fantastic!

Once we were admiring the view above Eilan Donan when another couple came beside us. The man was euphoric about the view, but his wife, wearing high heels said she was fed up with Scotland—it was nothing but lakes and mountains! She had wanted to go to Blackpool, apparently! It certainly takes all sorts!

One year we went to the north-west tip of Sutherland when we visited a craft village based in a collection of RAF Nissen Huts, a wartime signals station at Balnakeil. This was a community of people involved in weaving, candlemaking, carving and other suchlike pursuits. A very windy place on the edge of the cliffs. On this trip we also took the small ferry across the Kyle of Durness to join a minibus across the wild landscape to Cape Wrath lighthouse. As there were no other vehicles in that part of the world the driver went like there was no tomorrow round boulders, sheep and over fords. The views from the top of the cliffs were awesome and very vertiginous.

On another occasion we took a boat trip from Oban to view Fingal's Cave on Staffa but the weather closed in and we didn't get so much as a glance through the fog. Also the very loud foghorn made Joan feel ill and we did not even leave the boat to visit Iona.

We also visited various "brochs", ancient round stone buildings built to house people and cattle during raids by Vikings. There was room in the very thick walls to shelter people—and the entrance was so arranged that only one person could attempt to enter at a time—to his acute embarrassment when meeting a reception committee no doubt armed with something very sharp!

In those days there was a climate of courtesy on the roads, which has completely vanished in the present attitude of most drivers to resent the presence of anybody else. On the single track roads in the Highlands there were passing places, and it was the rule (voluntary) for the first vehicle to reach the place to pull in and let the other vehicle pass. This was always done with a cheery wave and a "Thanks". And if you met someone driving the same model car as yours, it was almost like meeting a relation!

In the motor cars, we have gone from the Ruby EUL 956, to Morris 10, DOU 616; Isis, VPO 967; Vauxhall Victor, 544 LBP; Viva Estate, XBP 260 F; Viva Saloon, ABP

757 L; Toyota Corolla, ETP 236 W; Volvo 340, FTR 812 D; and finally now Ford Escort, N 566 GOT.

(The Ruby cost £75), which doesn't seem like a lot of money these days, but it was a considerable amount in 1957. It gave us a mobility, which had been lacking, and enabled us to get about and see places we had only heard of.

WOODWORK

When I retired I built my workshop and was at last able to start doing the woodwork I had wanted to do as a youngster, lathe work and whatever—bowls, table lamps, candlesticks, trinket boxes, light pulls, stool legs, vases and a host of other things. Every visitor went away with a "lump of wood".

Having obtained all the tools and equipment I longed for in past years, it is unfortunate that health problems have made me cut down on the time I can spend in the workshop, but I still manage to do various jobs, especially when Tony, our neighbour wants the odd bit of wood worked in peculiar shapes for goodness knows what purpose.

I was very pleased to make a large bowl out of Horse Chestnut for a dear lady in the big house opposite, Mrs. Scrivenor, when one of her trees was trimmed, especially

Douglas Smith

as she was ill, and died just a few weeks afterwards. People had always moaned about her trees so she was thrilled to find that someone appreciated them. We met her son later on and he said he would cherish the bowl in memory of his mother.

COMPUTING

Now the dreaded Computer has taken over and my time is spent Emailing Rosalind, my sisters and friends, churning out greeting cards for every possible occasion, writing letters, sending Emails to the various TV letter pages and fighting off viruses with the aid of Norton Anti-Virus.

This machine would have reduced our work in Radar by quite a lot, but hey, that's Life.

THE END (Almost)

A Tribute

At Wing HQ there was a chap
Who was always pouring over a map.
Though some folks thought he was a myth
He was real flesh and blood was A. D. Smith.

A draughtsman he professed to be,
A Group one trade with appendix "G";
His weapons consisted of T-square and rule,
Dividers, protractor and engraving tool.

A draughtsman you know is a real learned man
Who works everything out according to plan:
So our Dougie when he first joined up in this trade
Was quite unaware of the blunder he'd made.

Douglas Smith

In the Service he was just a "last three, rank, name",
A mere pawn in the RAF's inexplicable game
Which is played up near Whitehall in large airy flats
By some big-wigs who wear scrambled egg on their hats.

Thus when he came out to S.E.A.,
And at 182 was told to stay,
His mind was full of gears and things,
Perspective and plan views, of cambers, chords, wings.

This marked the parting of the ways,
From the intricate draughting of those byegone days;
For now he was shown by some queer Radar chaps
Two almiras containing a few thousand maps.

Your work will be "secret so mind how you go

Your job in the future will be with these 'ere",

Said a person who wore a most horrible leer;

And only refer to those `men in the know`."

"And also you'll have perspex masks to prepare

And engrave with a coastline and grids here and there.

There will also be rulers and scales to be made

Thus `improvisator `will be your new trade."

On hearing this our Dougie Smith

Began to wish he were a myth.

His dreams as a draughtsman crashed to the ground

As the map making piled up to form quite a mound.

Douglas Smith

For day in and day out and night-time he worked,
At the back of his mind a small hope there still lurked
That at some future time fate would smile and be kind
He'd be back drawing blueprints with peace in his mind.

But as D-day grew near, the Command soon found out
That without Dougie's maps they'd be much put about
Thus realisation did come to our Doug.
He was no longer ex-draughtsman stuck deep in the mud.

From a pawn in the game he rose to a knight,
And when victory was won certain facts came to light;
On the lips of the world was the name of our myth—
Three O six one O six one A. Douglas Smith.

"With the compliments of my servile humility"
      "B. A. White

School Song

Here at school in early youth,
Where we learn to honour truth
While we strive with might and main
To do our best with hand and brain—
May our watchword ever be
True unswerving Loyalty

As we grow to manly power,
Getting wiser every hour
We'll treasure lessons learned today
To help our friends as best we may
And let our watchword always be
True unswerving Loyalty.

Through the years that lie ahead,

In whatever path we tread,

May memories of school return

To make our hearts within us burn

And through life our watchword be

True unswerving Loyalty

R. Bassett and H. Lamb

Lightning Source UK Ltd.
Milton Keynes UK
UKOW05n0319060114

224005UK00001B/15/P